CARDIFF
CAERDYDD

MAJOR
EUROPEAN UNION
NATIONS

Austria
Belgium
Czech Republic
Denmark
France
Germany
Greece
Ireland

Italy
The Netherlands
Poland
Portugal
Spain
Sweden
United Kingdom

Major European Union Nations

CZECH REPUBLIC

by
Heather Docalavich and Shaina C. Indovino

Mason Crest

Mason Crest
370 Reed Road, Broomall,
Pennsylvania 19008
www.masoncrest.com

Printed in the Hashemite Kingdom of Jordan.

First printing
9 8 7 6 5 4 3 2 1

Library of Congress Cataloging-in-Publication Data

Docalavich, Heather.
  The Czech Republic / by Heather Docalavich and Shaina C. Indovino.
      p. cm. — (The European Union : political, social, and economic cooperation)
  Includes bibliographical references and index.
  ISBN 978-1-4222-2237-9 (hardcover) — ISBN 978-1-4222-2231-7 (series hardcover) — ISBN 978-1-4222-9264-8 (ebook)
  1. Czech Republic—Juvenile literature. 2. European Union—Czech Republic—Juvenile literature. I. Indovino, Shaina Carmel. II. Title.
  DB2011.D63 2012
  943.7105—dc22
                                      201005108

Produced by Harding House Publishing Services, Inc.
www.hardinghousepages.com
Interior layout by Micaela Sanna.
Cover design by Torque Advertising + Design.

Contents

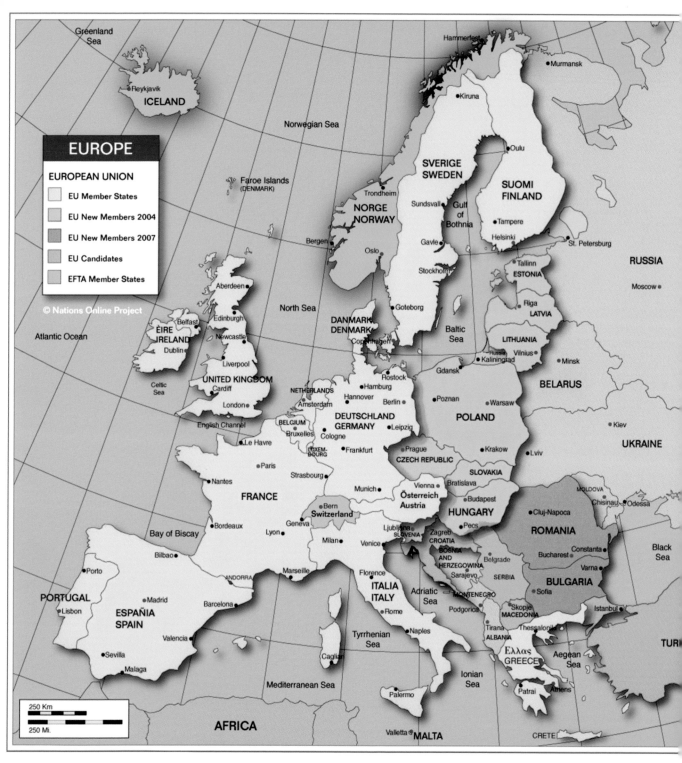

CZECH REPUBLIC
European Union Member since 2004

Liberec

Teplice · Ustí
nad Labdem

Karlovy
Vary

Klando

⭐ Prague

Hradec
Králové

Pardubice

Krnov

Haviřov

Pilsen · Rokycany

Ostrava

Příbram

Olomouc

Frýdek-Místek

Havlíčkuv

Prostějov

Tábor

Kroměříž

Brno

Zlín

Uherské
Hradiste

Ceské ·
Budějovice

INTRODUCTION

Sixty years ago, Europe lay scarred from the battles of the Second World War. During the next several years, a plan began to take shape that would unite the countries of the European continent so that future wars would be inconceivable. On May 9, 1950, French Foreign Minister Robert Schuman issued a declaration calling on France, Germany, and other European countries to pool together their coal and steel production as "the first concrete foundation of a European federation." "Europe Day" is celebrated each year on May 9 to commemorate the beginning of the European Union (EU).

The EU consists of twenty-seven countries, spanning the continent from Ireland in the west to the border of Russia in the east. Eight of the ten most recently admitted EU member states are former communist regimes that were behind the Iron Curtain for most of the latter half of the twentieth century.

Any European country with a democratic government, a functioning market economy, respect for fundamental rights, and a government capable of implementing EU laws and policies may apply for membership. Bulgaria and Romania joined the EU in 2007. Croatia, Serbia, Turkey, Iceland, Montenegro, and Macedonia have also embarked on the road to EU membership.

While the EU began as an idea to ensure peace in Europe through interconnected economies, it has evolved into so much more today:

- Citizens can travel freely throughout most of the EU without carrying a passport and without stopping for border checks.

- EU citizens can live, work, study, and retire in another EU country if they wish.

- The euro, the single currency accepted throughout seventeen of the EU countries (with more to come), is one of the EU's most tangible achievements, facilitating commerce and making possible a single financial market that benefits both individuals and businesses.

- The EU ensures cooperation in the fight against cross-border crime and terrorism.

- The EU is spearheading world efforts to preserve the environment.

- As the world's largest trading bloc, the EU uses its influence to promote fair rules for world trade, ensuring that globalization also benefits the poorest countries.

- The EU is already the world's largest donor of humanitarian aid and development assistance, providing around 60 percent of global official development assistance to developing countries in 2011.

The EU is not a nation intended to replace existing nations. The EU is unique—its member countries have established common institutions to which they delegate some of their sovereignty so that decisions on matters of joint interest can be made democratically at the European level.

Europe is a continent with many different traditions and languages, but with shared values such as democracy, freedom, and social justice, cherished values well known to North Americans. Indeed, the EU motto is "United in Diversity."

Enjoy your reading. Take advantage of this chance to learn more about Europe and the EU!

Ambassador John Bruton,
Former EU President and Prime Minister of Ireland

Prague, the Czech Republic's capital city

1 Modern Issues

The Czech Republic has seen a lot in its time. This nation is in the geographic center of Europe, surrounded by land on all sides. It shares its borders with Poland, Germany, Austria, and Slovakia. Until fairly recently, the Czech Republic, together with Slovakia, made up one country—Czechoslovakia.

THE FORMATION OF THE EUROPEAN UNION

The EU is a confederation of European nations that continues to grow. All countries that enter the EU agree to follow common laws about foreign security policies. They also agree to cooperate on legal matters that go on within the EU. The European Council meets to discuss all international matters and make decisions about them. Each country's own concerns and interests are important, though. And apart from legal and financial issues, the EU tries to uphold values such as peace and solidarity, human dignity, freedom, and equality. All member countries remain autonomous. This means that they generally keep their own laws and regulations. The EU becomes involved only if there is an international issue or if a member country has violated the principles of the union.

The idea for a union among European nations was first mentioned after World War II. The war had devastated much of Europe, both physically and financially. In 1950, French foreign minister Robert Schuman suggested that France and West Germany combine their coal and steel industries under one authority. Both countries would have control over the industries. This would help them become more financially stable. It would also make war between the countries much more difficult. The idea was interesting to other European countries as well. In 1951, France, West Germany, Belgium, Luxembourg, the Netherlands, and Italy signed the Treaty of Paris, creating the European Coal and Steel Community. These six countries would become the core of the EU.

In 1957, these same countries signed the Treaties of Rome, creating the European Economic Community. This combined their economies into a single European economy. In 1965, the Merger Treaty brought together a number of these treaty organizations. The organizations were joined under a common banner, known as the European Community. Finally, in 1992, the Maastricht Treaty was signed. This treaty defined the European Union. It gave a framework for expanding the EU's political role, particularly in the area of foreign and security policy. It would also replace national currencies with the euro. The next year, the treaty went into effect. At that time, the member countries included the original six plus another six who had joined during the 1970s and '80s.

In the following years, the EU would take more steps to form a single market for its members. This would make joining the union even more of an advantage. Three more countries joined during the 1990s. Another twelve joined in the first decade of the twenty-first century. As of 2012, six more countries were waiting to join the EU.

Flags of the European Union.

Czechoslovakia was deeply involved in both world wars. Both wars resulted in its territory being seized and its borders altered several times. Throughout the later decades of the twentieth century, the Soviet Union ruled the country. In 1990, a free election was held for the first time in over forty years.

In 1993, Czechoslovakia split into two countries. The two newly formed countries became the Czech Republic and Slovakia. This separation

Who Are the Roma?

About a thousand years ago, groups of people migrated from northern India, spreading across Europe over the next several centuries. Though these people actually came from several different tribes (the largest of which were the Sinti and Roma), the people of Europe called them simply "Gypsies"—a shortened version of "Egyptians," since people thought they came from Egypt.

Europeans were frightened of these dark-skinned, non-Christian people who spoke a foreign language. Unlike the settled people of Europe, the Roma were wanderers, with no ties to the land. Europeans did not understand them. Stories and stereotypes grew up about the Gypsies, and these fanned the flames of prejudice and discrimination. Many of these same stories and stereotypes are still believed today.

Throughout the centuries, non-Gypsies continually tried to either assimilate the Gypsies or kill them. Attempts to assimilate the Gypsies involved stealing their children and placing them with other families; giving them cattle and feed, expecting them to become farmers; outlawing their customs, language, and clothing, and forcing them to attend school and church. In many ways the Roma of Europe were treated much as the European settlers treated the Native peoples of North America.

Many European laws allowed—or even commanded—the killing of Gypsies. A practice of "Gypsy hunting"—similar to fox hunting—was both common and legal in some parts of Europe. Even as late as 1835, a Gypsy hunt in Denmark "brought in a bag of over 260 men, women, and children." But the worst of all crimes against the Roma happened in the twentieth century, when Hitler's Third Reich sent them to concentration camps. As many as half a million Gypsies died in the Nazis' death camps.

was mostly due to differences in political opinions and cultural heritage. It made more sense for Czechs and Slovaks to have their own nations, rather than to be forced to live under one rule.

Today, these countries thrive as separate entities, rejuvenated by their independence from each other. However, plenty of problems always come along with being an immature nation. Having only been officially formed less than twenty years ago, the Czech Republic lacks the experience that other nations of Europe have.

Dividing from another nation is not always an easy transition. Joining NATO in 1999 and the European Union in 2004 has helped the Czech Republic tremendously. However, there are still challenges that the country faces. These include navigating the current economic crisis, increasing the government's ***transparency***, improving housing, reforming healthcare, protecting the environment, and protecting the rights of minorities.

The Roma

The world community frequently criticizes the Czech Republic for the way it treats the Roma who live within its borders. The Roma—also known as

Gypsies—are an ancient group of people who have been in Europe for hundreds, if not thousands, of years. These people face **prejudice** and *discrimination* in many European nations, but their lives are particularly hard in the Czech Republic.

About 188,000 Roma live in the Czech Republic. Many times they are forced to live in areas that are kept separate from other Czechs. The Czech Republic is known for separating Roma children into "special schools" and "special classes." Nearly 40 percent of Roma children drop out

With such limited educational oppurtunities, the Roma often live out their entire lives in poverty.

MUSLIMS IN THE EUROPEAN UNION

Muslims are people who follow Islam, a religion that grew from some of the same roots as Judaism and Christianity. "Islam" means "submission to God," and Muslims try to let God shape all aspects of their lives. They refer to God as Allah; their holy scriptures are called the Qur'an, and they consider the Prophet Muhammad to be their greatest teacher.

About 16 million Muslims live in the European Union—but their stories vary from country to country. Some Muslim populations have been living in Europe for hundreds of years. Others came in the middle of the twentieth century. Still others are recent refugees from the troubled Middle East. By 2020, the Muslim population in Europe is predicted to double. By 2050, one in five Europeans are likely to be Muslim, and by 2100, Muslims may make up one-quarter of Europe's people.

Not all Europeans are happy about these predictions. Negative stereotypes about Muslims are common in many EU countries. Some Europeans think all Muslims are terrorists. But stereotypes are dangerous!

When you believe a stereotype, you think that people in a certain group all act a certain way. "All jocks are dumb" is a stereotype. "All women are emotional" is another stereotype, and another is, "All little boys are rough and noisy." Stereotypes aren't true! And when we use stereotypes to think about others, we often fall into prejudice—thinking that some groups of people aren't as good as others.

Fundamentalist Muslims want to get back to the fundamentals—the basics—of Islam. However, their definition of what's "fundamental" is not always the same as other Muslims'. Generally speaking, they are afraid that the influence of Western morals and values will be bad for Muslims. They believe that the laws of Islam's holy books should be followed literally. Many times, they are willing to kill for their beliefs—and they are often willing to die for them as well. Men and women who are passionate about these beliefs have taken part in violent attacks against Europe and the United States. They believe that terrorism will make the world take notice of them, that it will help them fight back against the West's power.

But most Muslims are not terrorists. In fact, most Muslims are law-abiding and hardworking citizens of the countries where they live. Some Muslims, however, believe that women should have few of the rights that women expect in most countries of the EU. This difference creates tension, since the EU guarantees women the same rights as men.

But not all Muslims are so conservative and strict. Many of them believe in the same "golden rule" preached by all major religions: "Treat everyone the way you want to be treated."

But despite this, hate crimes against Muslims are increasing across the EU. These crimes range from death threats and murder to more minor assaults, such as spitting and name-calling. Racism against Muslims is a major problem in many parts of the EU. The people of the European Union must come to terms with the fact that Muslims are a part of them now. Terrorism is the enemy to be fought—not Muslims.

of school before they complete their elementary education. Out of thousands of Roma young people, only a handful will even go to high school. With such poor educational opportunities, many Roma children are destined to repeat their parents' lives of poverty.

MUSLIMS

Muslims are another group that sometimes faces prejudice in the Czech Republic. However, in many cases Muslims are readily accepted in the country.

Since 1912, Islam has been recognized in this region as a state religion, and its presence was officially allowed. In 1998 a mosque was opened in Brno and a year later in Prague. Attempts to open mosques in a couple of other cities was stopped, however, by local citizens who did not welcome the growth of Islam in their midst. In 2004, Islam was officially registered, which means the Muslim community is now eligible to obtain funds from the government.

Most of the Muslims in the Czech Republic today migrated there from Bosnia-Herzegovina early in the 1990s, as well as from former countries of the Soviet Union in the late 1990s until the present. Many are middle-class people of Egyptian, Syrian, and other Middle Eastern ancestries who came to study in Czechoslovakia and decided to stay. A few hundred Muslims in the Czech Republic are Czech converts. Most Czechs tend not to be very religious, and Christianity is not thriving there. By contrast, Islam offers a living faith tradition that appeals to some Czechs.

In 2006, however, prejudice against Muslims in the country was fueled when Islamic terrorists conspired to hold Jews hostage in a Prague synagogue and then blow up the building. The 2006, Prague terror plot was foiled by Czech security services.

OTHER CURRENT DISPUTES

The Czech Republic has been the center of local controversy in recent years. Austrian citizens have become outspoken about a nuclear power plant in Temelín, a Czech village close to the Austrian border. A petition was signed in 2008 stating that the Czech Republic should be removed from the European Union if the nuclear power plant was not shut down.

Plenty of Czech citizens also showed their distaste for the power plant, but nothing was changed. In time, the Czech Republic hopes to rely less on nuclear energy and more on renewable energy sources. This would help remedy this problem. As of 2012, however, the nuclear power plant remained open, with plans to expand.

View of Prague, the center of the Czech Republic's government.

2 CHAPTER
THE CZECH REPUBLIC'S HISTORY AND GOVERNMENT

The country we recognize today as the Czech Republic is a new nation, formed on January 1, 1993, when the former Czechoslovakia separated, creating two new countries—the Czech Republic and Slovakia. Although the Czech Republic is an infant nation, its land and people have a rich and ancient history.

Czech Lands in Ancient Times

Human settlement of modern-day Czech lands was first recorded around 400 BCE, with the arrival of Celts from Western Europe. Ancient Romans called the region "Boiohaemum" after the Boii Celts who occupied the area. This name stuck, as people still refer to the western region of the Czech Republic as "Bohemia." Although the Boii were partially chased out of the region by invading Germanic tribes, they left a lasting influence on the culture and language of the area. One example is the Czech name for the Moldau River, which runs through the capital city of Prague. Czechs call the river "Vltava," which is said to have come from the Celtic words "Vit" and "Va," meaning "wild" and "water."

By 600 CE, Slavic people fully inhabited the area, having migrated in waves from the east. A century later, a Frankish merchant named Samo united the people of the territory into the first recorded state. This early state collapsed shortly after Samo's death, and the area remained unstable until the ninth century. Czechs were next briefly united with their Slovak neighbors as part of the Great Moravian Empire, established by the Slavic leader Mojmir. Around this time, the Przemyslid family established the Bohemian Kingdom, joining the various Czech tribes in Bohemia, Moravia, and Silesia under stable *feudal* rule.

The Bohemian Kingdom

As the Great Moravian Empire disintegrated, a new state known as the kingdom of Bohemia emerged by the tenth century. It would play an important role in the development of the Czech nation. The Bohemian Kingdom was a major medieval political, economic, and cultural entity and is now viewed by many Czechs as one of the brightest periods of their country's history.

Dating Systems and Their Meaning

You might be accustomed to seeing dates expressed with the abbreviations BC or AD, as in the year 1000 BC or the year AD 1900. For centuries, this dating system has been the most common in the Western world. However, since BC and AD are based on Christianity (BC stands for Before Christ and AD stands for *anno Domini*, Latin for "in the year of our Lord"), many people now prefer to use abbreviations that people from all religions can be comfortable using. The abbreviations BCE (meaning Before Common Era) and CE (meaning Common Era), mark time in the same way (for example, 1000 BC is the same year as 1000 BCE and AD 1900 is the same year as 1900 CE), but BCE and CE do not have the same religious overtones as BC and AD.

Castles are reminders of the Czech Republic's ancient history.

Over the centuries, the Przemyslid family accumulated land, wealth, and power, eventually extending the Bohemian Kingdom from areas in modern-day Austria all the way to the Adriatic Sea. The young Przemyslid state maintained its **sovereignty**, even though it officially recognized the feudal authority of the Holy Roman Empire.

The Holy Roman Empire was a group of European territories that stood united by their common faith in the Roman Catholic Church, under the rule of one supreme emperor. Individual territories had their own rulers, each of whom acknowledged the authority of the emperor both through the payment of **tribute** and military alliances.

The Cathedral of St. Vitus in Prague is a reminder of the important role the church played in Czech history.

As the Bohemian Empire expanded, the Czech people were exposed to strong German and Roman Catholic influences through their allegiance to the empire. As the population swelled and trade flourished, Czech lands soon came to be counted among the richest of the European feudal states. And as the wealth of the region expanded, the Przemyslid family and the regional *nobility* sought to increase their power and independence.

In 1212, King Premysl Otakar I received the Golden Bull of Sicily (a formal decree) from the

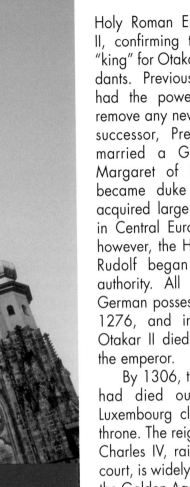

Holy Roman Emperor Frederick II, confirming the royal title of "king" for Otakar and his descendants. Previously, the emperor had the power to appoint or remove any new ruler. The king's successor, Premysl Otakar II, married a German princess, Margaret of Babenberg, and became duke of Austria and acquired large amounts of land in Central Europe. From 1273, however, the Hapsburg Emperor Rudolf began to reassert his authority. All Premysl Otakar's German possessions were lost in 1276, and in 1278, Premysl Otakar II died in battle against the emperor.

By 1306, the Przemyslid line had died out, and John of Luxembourg claimed the Czech throne. The reign of his son, King Charles IV, raised in the French court, is widely acknowledged as the Golden Age of Czech history. Charles IV was crowned Holy Roman Emperor in 1355. The Bohemian Kingdom ceased to be a **fief** of the emperor, and Prague became the new imperial city. During his reign as King of Bohemia, Charles had implemented building projects over the entire region, including a major renovation of Hradcany, the royal castle. Charles University was founded in 1348 and helped cement Prague's status as a leading international center of culture and learning.

In the centuries that followed, the Czech people endured great political and religious upheaval. This period, during which the **Protestant Reformation** swept across Europe, saw a series of anti-Catholic and anti-German revolts as people began to question the authority of the Roman Catholic Church. A sizable number of Germans had migrated to the region during the growth of the Bohemian Empire, and now cultural and ethnic differences between Germans and Czechs added fuel to religious conflicts.

Czechs opposed to the practices of the Catholic Church were known as *Hussites*, after the early Czech reformer Jan Hus, who was burned at the stake by Catholics for his views. The Hussite movement gained momentum, and its followers eventually defeated five separate waves of Catholic **crusaders**—before they began warring with one another over economic and social divisions.

The political situation was very volatile, and power would change hands many times before stable, effective rule was eventually reestablished. This began when Bohemia first came under the rule of the Hapsburg family of Austria. Although the first Hapsburg ruler, King Ferdinand, took control of the Bohemian throne in 1526, rebellion and religious wars continued to plague the territory until Hapsburg forces decisively defeated Czech troops at the Battle of White Mountain on November 8, 1620.

Hapsburg Rule

The Hapsburg victory over Czech forces in 1620 was followed by strict new measures that ensured the **absolute rule** of the Hapsburg Dynasty and the supremacy of the Roman Catholic Church in the region. All Czech lands were declared hereditary property of the Hapsburg family, and all law was issued by royal decree. Many native Czech nobles were executed; most of the rest fled, their lands confiscated by the crown.

Many German Catholics immigrated to the area and became the new Bohemian nobility. The entire educational system, including Charles University, was placed under Catholic control. German became the dominant language of the region. The Hapsburg policy of **centralization** ultimately cost the Czechs most of their native aristocracy, their reformed religion, and even the common use of their native language.

By the eighteenth century, all that remained of the Bohemian kingdom had been merged into the Austrian provinces of the Hapsburg realm. During this period, known as the **Age of Enlightenment**, Europe saw remarkable cultural changes characterized by a loss of faith in traditional religious sources of authority and a turn toward human rights, science, and rational thought. Hapsburg rulers Maria-Theresa and her son Joseph II instituted reforms based on Enlightenment principles to promote social and economic progress.

The significant consequences of Enlightment reforms were widespread. The power and author-ity of the Catholic Church were reduced, and some freedom of worship was established. Catholic control of education came to a halt, and the focus of study shifted from **theology** to the sciences. Feudalism was modified, so **serfs** could marry and change residences without obtaining the lord's consent.

Eventually the nobility shifted its focus from agriculture to industry, investing their profits in coal mining and manufacture. This freed Czech peasants from the land, and saw the migration of workers from the countryside to urban centers. The sons of these peasants were educated, and for the first time some attended the university. The increased educational and economic opportunities presented by Enlightenment era reforms set the stage for a resurgence of Czech pride and culture.

Czech Nationalism

The dawn of the nineteenth century marked a period of national awakening across Central Europe. The aggression of the French general, Napoleon Bonaparte, created a wave of **nationalism** among Germans. The concept of a nation as a group of people linked by a common language and culture had great appeal to the Czech people who had lived for centuries under foreign rule. Inspired by the renewed interest in German national identity that was taking place among their neighbors, the Czech intellectual **elite** soon launched a national revival of their own.

Initial national movements were limited to discussions of language, literature, and culture. The

Karlstejn Castle near Prague was the home of Czech nobility.

Cultural elements like costume, language, and festivals helped build a sense of Czech nationalism.

Czech language, by this time, existed only as a peasant dialect. Scholars began their first attempts to record the Czech language and to introduce the study of Czech language in state schools. The Museum of the Bohemian Kingdom was established in 1818 and served as a center for Czech scholarly activity. Nationalist feeling soon expanded beyond scholarly pursuits, and Czech nationalists began to form political alliances as well. Czechs reached out to other Slavic peoples such as the Slovaks, Poles, Slovenians, Croats, Ukrainians, and Serbs with whom they shared a common ethnic identity.

By 1848, the Hapsburgs were seeing a series of nationalist demonstrations and revolts across their lands. In 1859 they were driven out of Italy, and by 1866, they were defeated by Germany and expelled from the German Confederation. To strengthen his political power base, Hapsburg Emperor Francis Joseph reached out to the Hungarian nobility and in 1867, created the Austro-Hungarian Empire. Austria and Hungary were now united by a common ruler but were otherwise independent states, each with a separate **parliament** and judicial system. Political power rested with ethnic Germans in Austria and Hungarians in Hungary. Czechs were eventually allowed greater political involvement in the Austrian half of the empire, which peaked when all men were given the right to vote in 1907. In neighboring Hungary, however, the Slovak population was continually denied the right to participate in their government.

WORLD WAR I AND THE CZECHOSLOVAK REPUBLIC

The inability of the Austro-Hungarian Empire to ease tensions between the different nationalities under its rule eventually led to the fall of the empire. World War I began on June 28, 1914, when Gavrilo Princip, a Serbian nationalist, assassinated Austrian Archduke Franz Ferdinand and his wife Sophie. Russia allied with Serbia. Germany sided with Austria and soon declared war on Russia. After France declared its support for Russia, Germany attacked France. German troops then invaded Belgium, a **neutral** country, as it stood between German forces and Paris. Great Britain declared war on Germany.

Czechs and Slovaks had little interest in fighting for their oppressors, the Germans and Hungarians, against Russians and Serbians who were fellow Slavs. Czech and Slovak troops deserted the German army on the Russian front and formed the Czechoslovak Legion. Germany and Austria proposed peace negotiations in early October 1918, and on October 28, 1918, the Czechoslovak National Council in Prague proclaimed the independence of Czechoslovakia.

When the Paris Peace Conference opened in January 1919, the provisional Czechoslovak government was represented. The victorious allies formally recognized the Czechoslovak Republic and established its borders. The new republic would cover the lands of the historic Bohemian kingdom, Slovakia, and an area called Ruthenia, thus gaining a common border with Romania. The new nation had a population of over 13.5 million. It also inherited between 70 and 80 percent of all industries formerly held by the Austro-Hungarian Empire, making the infant democracy one of the world's ten most industrialized states.

One problem that plagued the new republic was the dissatisfaction of the German minority. Once in control of much of the wealth, land, and political power of the region, the Germans resented their smaller role in the new government. Most of these Germans occupied a region known as the **Sudetenland**, on Czechoslovakia's western border. The grievances of this minority German population would come to serve as a **pretext** for the eventual Nazi takeover of Czechoslovakia.

An old cemetery in Prague is a memorial to the Czech Jewish population.

World War II and the Rise of Communism

By 1933, Adolph Hitler had come to power in nearby Germany, and by 1938, he had occupied neighboring Austria as well. His stated objective was to unify all ethnic Germans. He soon demanded the surrender of Czechoslovakia's Sudetenland, taking up the cause of the Sudeten Germans. On September 29, 1938, France, Germany, Italy, and Great Britain signed the Munich Agreement, demanding that Czechoslovakia surrender the Sudetenland to Germany in exchange for a promise of peace. However, in March 1939, Hitler **reneged** on his agreement and invaded the remainder of Czechoslovakia.

Czechoslovakia was reestablished in 1945, after the defeat of Nazi Germany. It retained all of its 1938 boundaries except for the province of Ruthenia, which was **ceded** to the Soviet Union. Although democracy was briefly reintroduced, the new government was unstable.

The Soviet Army was a strong presence in Eastern Europe in the years following World War II. Taking advantage of their great influence, communists maneuvered to gain political power by obtaining key government positions. By 1948, the Soviets had taken over completely, and Czechoslovakia was converted into a **satellite nation** of the Soviet Union. Under communism, all private ownership of land and industry was outlawed. Every aspect of Czech life was now under the direct control of the government.

Resistance and Reform

By the late 1960s, key changes had occurred in Czechoslovakian communist leadership. In March 1968, the Communist Party announced a **radical** policy of **liberalization** called "Socialism with a Human Face." The rapid spread of democratization that followed became known as the "Prague Spring." The Soviet Union acted quickly to put down the movement, sending 600,000 troops from neighboring communist countries to occupy Czechoslovakia and force an end to the movement. A harsh communist government was installed whose repressive policies were intended to prevent any further attempts at reform. This government would rule unchallenged for two decades.

Sweeping political changes were taking place across Eastern Europe by the late 1980s. Inspired by events in East Germany, Poland, and the Soviet Union itself, demonstrators swarmed the streets of Prague in November 1989, demanding political and economic reforms. This is known in Czech history as the "Velvet Revolution" due to the smooth transition of power and the fact that no blood was shed in earning Czech independence from Soviet control.

Prague's new hotel, image of the modern Czech Republic

In June 1990, free elections were held for the first time in forty-two years. By 1992, a democratic government had been established, and voters passed a **referendum** ending the political union of Czechs and Slovaks. On January 1, 1993, Czechoslovakia ceased to exist and the Czech Republic was born.

POLITICAL SHIFTS

Political opinions have mostly remained stable throughout the short time of the Czech Republic's existence. The two most represented parties are the Social Democratic Party and the Civic Democratic Party. Since the 1996 elections, these two parties have reigned supreme within the Czech parliament. The Social Democratic Party was not very popular when Czechoslovakia first split, but it has gained tremendous support since then. This may be because the party holds socialist *ideals*. The Civic Democratic Party leans more towards the right. These two parties make up for more than half of the seats within parliament.

By 2010, a new party had seats in parliament, the Traditional Responsibility Prosperity (TOP) 09 party. This party caused the top two parties to lose many seats in the 2010 election. It was formed in 2009, perhaps as a result of the recent economic crisis. It is considered to be a right-wing party, which branched off from the Christian and Democratic Union, a party that lost all of its seats in the 2010 elections as the TOP 09 party gained support.

Two other parties currently represented within parliament are the Communist Party and Public Affairs party. The first was founded when Czechoslovakia split. It was seen as a way to keep **communist** ideals alive within the new republic. It is not as popular as other parties but still has twenty-six seats in parliament. The Public Affairs party focuses on transparency and removing corruption from the government.

The current president of the Czech Republic is Václav Klaus. He has been in office since 2003 and was reelected in 2008. Klaus is a former prime minister, an office he held from 1992 to 1997. Klaus does not support a strong EU and favors the Czech Republic holding on to its separate authority.

An apothecary's shop in Prague

3 THE ECONOMY

O f all the developing democracies in Eastern Europe, the Czech Republic has one of the fastest-growing economies in the region. Since its independence from Soviet control, the Czech Republic has struggled to overcome the loss of favorable trade with former communist countries to the East, some of which still owe the former Czechoslovakia substantial debts. The Czech

Quick Facts: The Economy of the Czech Republic

Gross Domestic Product (GDP): US$272.2 billion (2011 est.)

GDP per capita: US$25,900 (2011 est.)

Industries: motor vehicles, metallurgy, machinery and equipment, glass, armaments

Agriculture: wheat, potatoes, sugar beets, hops, fruit; pigs, poultry

Export Commodities: machinery and transport equipment, raw materials and fuel, chemicals

Export Partners: Germany 31.7%, Slovakia 8.7%, Poland 6.2%, France 5.5%, UK 4.9%, Austria 4.7%, Italy 4.5% (2010 est.)

Import Commodities: machinery and transport equipment, raw materials and fuels, chemicals

Import Partners: Germany 25.6%, China 11.9%, Poland 6.5%, Russia 5.4%, Slovakia 5.2% (2010 est.)

Currency: Czech koruny (CZK)

Currency Exchange Rate: US $1=14.25 CZK (March 2012 est.)

Note: All figures are from 2011 unless otherwise noted.
Source: www.cia.gov, 2012.

---

chemical production, transportation equipment, textiles, glass, brewing, electronics, china, ceramics, and medical drugs. The country has a strong industrial heritage dating back to the days when Bohemia was a major industrial base. Unfortunately, although the nation has an educated, capable workforce and a solid **infrastructure**, many of its factories were neglected while the communists were in control. More foreign investment is needed to bring facilities and equipment up to date.

Republic has been emerging from a **recession** since 1999, but is now well on its way to economic recovery, despite the economic problems of many EU states.

A Developing Economy

Primary industries in the Czech Republic remain much the same today as under communism. Heavy and general machine building makes up the largest sector of industry, followed closely by iron and steel production, metalworking,

Agriculture

The Czech Republic is now primarily an urban industrial society rather than an **agrarian** one. Farming today is mainly used to meet local demand, and currently makes up only 3 percent of the total **gross domestic product (GDP)**.

The leading crops produced are sugar beets, potatoes, wheat, and hops for the thriving domestic brewing industry.

ENERGY SOURCES

Heavily dependent on polluting brown coal as a source of energy, the Czech government is investing in developing cleaner, more efficient sources of energy. Currently, about 25 percent of the country's energy needs are met through nuclear power, although that figure is expected to rise as high as 40 percent in the near future. Natural gas is also a critical source of energy, and the country currently imports most of its gas via pipelines from Norway and Russia. Oil is imported from foreign lands as well.

The Czech Republic has a growing infrastructure, including city trains.

The central railway station in Prague

TRANSPORTATION

Transportation in the Czech Republic is mainly via highway or rail. The country's three **navigable** rivers—the Elbe, the Vltava, and the Oder—also provide water transportation. Air travel is available at forty-four airports across the nation.

A SHIFT IN TRADE AND INVESTMENT

Profound changes have been made in all aspects of the Czech economy. A conscious effort has been made to look to the West rather than toward the old economic partners in the East for investment and trade. Significant improvements have been made in the areas of telecommunications and banking to facilitate foreign investment in Czech enterprise, and business laws and practices have been overhauled to meet Western standards.

The new republic has successfully managed to **privatize** most of the country's industries through a unique voucher program. With the voucher system, each citizen has an opportunity to buy, at an affordable price, a book of industrial vouchers. Each voucher represents a potential share in a previously state-owned company. Holders then invest their vouchers in a specific company, providing needed money, which in turn helps to increase the stability of the company and the economic value of each individual share. When this privatization process is complete, the Czech people will own large shares in most of the major industries in the country, making them some of the highest **per capita** shareholders in the world.

Domestic demand is also playing an important role in fueling the expansion of the Czech economy. Credit cards and mortgages have become more easily available, and interest rates are beginning to fall, creating an increased demand for housing, consumer goods, and services. In fact, according to a 2011 estimate, service industries make up almost 60 percent of the GDP.

Although some problems persist, the Czech Republic has become one of the most prosperous states in Eastern Europe. Recent growth has been accelerated through an increase in exports to the EU, and foreign investment in Czech enterprise has nearly doubled in recent years. Continued governmental restructuring of banking, communications, and utilities will be needed to ensure continued economic development.

GLOBAL RECESSION

In 2007, the United States' economy went into a tailspin. The country plunged into a recession that soon spread to the rest of the world. By 2008, the European Union was facing its own economic crisis. None of its member countries were immune.

The Czech Republic's economy stayed strong at first. When economies are linked as closely as the EU's nations are, however, once one goes, they are all bound to topple like dominoes. The Czech Republic's once thriving businesses began to suffer. Unemployment rates rose. Along with the rest of Europe, the nation struggled to emerge from the recession. But it takes time to turn things around. So far, it looks like it has. GDP growth recovered and looks like it will continue.

One of Prague's quiet streets in the Charles Bridge area

4 THE CZECH REPUBLIC'S PEOPLE AND CULTURE

Most of the more than ten million people living in the Czech Republic today can identify themselves as ethnic Czechs. Moravians, Slovaks, Poles, Germans, Silesians, Hungarians, and Roma (often called Gypsies) make up the non-Czech minority. The country's official language is Czech, and the Czech people are highly literate. Daily life in the Czech Republic looks much like life across Western Europe, and the people are very fond of literature, music, and the arts.

RELIGION

People living in the Czech Republic today enjoy full freedom of religion. Historically, Christianity was the dominant faith in the region, although this changed when the area came under communist control. Under communism, all public practice of religion was outlawed. It is no wonder that today, after forty years of enforced atheism, almost 40 percent of Czechs still identify themselves as atheists. Nearly as many identify themselves as Roman Catholics, while the remainder of the population is primarily undecided or affiliated with a Protestant faith. A small community of Czech Jews also exists. Estimated at about 10,000 people, most of this Jewish community is centered in the famous Josefov district of Prague. It is estimated that as many as 360,000 Jews were settled in Czech lands prior to the Nazi invasion of World War II.

QUICK FACTS: THE PEOPLE OF THE CZECH REPUBLIC

Population: 10,177,300 (July 2012 est.)

Ethnic Groups: Czech 90.4%, Moravian 3.7%, Slovak 1.9%, other 4% (2001 census)

Age Structure:
   0–14 years: 13.5%
   15–64 years: 70.2%
   65 years and over: 16.3% (2011 est.)

Population Growth Rate: –0.134% (2012 est.)

Birth Rate: 8.62 births/1,000 population (2012 est.)

Death Rate: 10.94 deaths/1,000 population (July 2012 est.)

Migration Rate: 0.97 migrant(s)/1,000 population (2012 est.)

Infant Mortality Rate: 3.7 deaths/1,000 live births

Life Expectancy at Birth:
   Total Population: 77.38 years
   Male: 74.11 years
   Female: 80.83 years (2012 est.)

Total Fertility Rate: 1.27 children born/woman (2012 est.)

Religions: Roman Catholic 26.8%, Protestant 2.1%, other 3.3%, unspecified 8.8%, unaffiliated 59% (2001 census)

Languages: Czech 94.9%, Slovak 2%, other 2.3%, unidentified 0.8% (2001 census)

Literacy Rate: 99.9%

Note: All figures are from 2011 unless otherwise noted.
Source: www.cia.gov, 2012.

FOOD AND DRINK: SIMPLE FARE AND LOCAL BREWS

Most traditional Czech meals consist of meat served with potatoes, dumplings, or cabbage. Beef and pork are favorites, and they are most commonly served fried or roasted. Typical eating habits feature a light breakfast and evening meal, with the main meal being

Colorful costumes at a Slavic festival in Moravia

served for lunch in the middle of the day. Some favorite national dishes include:

Svickova: a beef pot roast served in a creamy vegetable sauce with dumplings
Bramboraky: deep-fried potato pancakes
Knedlo Vepro Zelo: pork with dumplings and cabbage

As far as beverages are concerned, a popular Czech proverb says it all: *"Kde se pivo vari, tam se dobre dari"*—"Where beer is brewed, they have it good." Czechs are the largest per-capita drinkers of beer in the world, consuming on average the equivalent of one bottle of beer for every man, woman, and child in the Czech Republic every day. Beer drinking was one of the few leisure activities to remain legal under communism, and the nation remains very proud of its beer industry.

Archaeological evidence suggests that hops, the critical ingredient for producing beer, were being cultivated in Czech lands as early as 859 CE and were being exported by 903 CE. By the eighteenth century, the world's first beer brewing textbook was written by Czech brewer, Frantisek Ondrej Poupe, a pioneer in many aspects of beer production. Breweries around the world later adopted his methods, including the introduction of thermometers and other scientific gauges to the brewing process.

Beer drinking is a central element of Czech culture. Pubs and country inns provide a place for friends to meet and a forum in which to discuss everything from hockey to politics. Most pubs feature only local brews; foreign imports make up less than 1 percent of total Czech consumption. Czechs are fiercely loyal to their own national brews, some of which have been produced locally for centuries. One popular Czech brand, Budvar (pronounced like the similarly named American brew, Budweiser) has been a favorite of Czech royalty and common people alike since the sixteenth century. The word Pilsener, a common term for a broad range of classic, darker beers, actually comes from the Czech town of Plzen. Today, a house in downtown Plzen is home to the world's oldest beer museum.

EDUCATION AND SPORTS: A LITERATE AND COMPETITIVE SOCIETY

Czechs are a highly literate people. More than 99 percent of adults can read and write, and most of those adults are able to speak more than one language. National pride runs deep, fueling a trend toward building a competitive edge in both the arenas of education and athletics.

This drive to be more competitive with the rest of the Western world has spurred a comprehensive reform of the Czech educational system.

Busy Wenceslas Square in Prague

Since 2003, changes have been made to bring all schools nationwide into compliance with a new set of academic standards and streamlined educational funding and administration. All children between three and six years of age can attend free nursery school, called *mateøská skola*. The majority of Czech children do attend, although attendance is not **compulsory** until age six. Then all children attend primary school, called *základni skola*, until age eleven. At age eleven, students have the option of studying at one of three different types of schools. *Gymnázium*, which is similar to college-bound high schools in the United States, is the school of choice for the

An ethnic festival in Straznice in Moravia

top 10 percent of Czech students. By law, class size in the *Gymnázium* is limited to thirty students or less, and the curriculum is determined by strict national standards. Other students may opt to attend a technical school, *støedni odborná skola,* or a vocational school, *støední odborné uèilistí.*

National pride is evident in the way Czechs approach competitive sports as well. In 1998, the Czech Republic National Hockey Team won Olympic gold, earning them the nickname the "Golden Boys of Nagano." The current national team is ranked as one of the top in the world.

Soccer, known as *fotbal*, is hugely popular with Czech fans. Pavel Nedved, a native Czech, has been voted European Player of the Year. Tennis, track and field events, cycling, and skiing are also favorites among Czech fans.

FESTIVALS AND EVENTS: SPIRITED AND IMAGINATIVE CELEBRATIONS

Holidays and festivals in the Czech Republic are celebrated with great enthusiasm. Traditional holidays reflect the diverse influences that have molded Czech culture through the centuries.

The Czech government honors eight national holidays. Some of these, like New Year's Day, Labor Day, Independence Day, and Christmas, are not celebrated much differently in the Czech Republic than they are in other countries. Easter is a national holiday, but unlike the United States, the Czech Republic celebrates Easter Monday. On Easter Monday a special custom called *Pomlázka* is observed, where men swat their favorite women with decorated willow switches. This is supposed to bring new life to the land. Then little boys visit all the little girls they know and beg for gifts of candy and painted eggs. Later in the day, adult men go around to all the women in the village, but instead of candy, they receive shots of alcohol.

Other festivals are important to Czech culture but are not recognized as official government holidays. These include the Burning of the Witches, held each year in April, and the Festival Jiein, held in September.

Czech Sports Legends
- Martina Navratilova—tennis
- Ivan Lendl—tennis
- Pavel Nedved—soccer
- Dominic Hasek—hockey
- Jaromir Jagr—hockey

The Burning of the Witches is a pre-Christian festival where all-night bonfires are held to drive evil spirits out of the land. September's Festival Jiein, is a weeklong celebration that starts with a costumed parade. At the end of the parade, the mayor of the town holds a ceremony where he turns the town over to the children to run for the next week. Plays, concerts, parties, and educational exhibits are held throughout the festival, which ends with a fireworks display.

ARTS AND ARCHITECTURE

Due in large part to Prague's place in history as a bridge between East and West, a wide variety of art and architecture is on display throughout the city. Historic cathedrals stand side by side with gleaming modern structures along the city skyline. Across the countryside, the Czech Republic boasts more than two thousand preserved or restored

The ceiling of Hluboka Castle

castles and chateaux, more than any other country in the world. These historic structures are an important piece of cultural heritage, and the government has taken important steps to preserve these national treasures while ensuring that they are largely open to the public.

MUSIC, FILM, AND LITERATURE: NOTABLE CONTRIBUTIONS

The Czech Republic has produced many notable talents whose work has left a lasting mark on the world stage.

Czech writers have made lasting contributions to world literature. Perhaps the best known Czech author is Franz Kafka. Kafka's haunting works, including *Metamorphosis* and *The Trial*, have become classics of literature studied and interpreted in schools around the world. Milan Kundera, best known for his book *The Unbearable Lightness of Being*, is recognized as one of the best contemporary writers in the world. Playwright Václav Havel was elected president of Czechoslovakia in 1989 and in 1993 became the first president of the Czech Republic.

Czechs today enjoy music of all styles, including hip-hop, rock, and most other types of popular music. Historically, Czech culture has produced many great composers throughout history. The most widely recognized is the classical composer Antonin Dvorak.

Czechs have been successful in more modern artistic pursuits as well. Josef Sudek is known for his groundbreaking work in photography. Milos Forman has received two Academy Awards for his work as a director. Forman received wide acclaim for his films *One Flew Over the Cuckoo's Nest* and *Amadeus*.

Clearly, the Czech Republic has as much to offer culturally as it does geographically and economically.

Town of Czech Krumlov, Czech Republic.

5 LOOKING TO THE FUTURE

Despite its long cultural history, the Czech Republic is a very new country. In fact, it is a mere teenager, not even twenty years old!

This folklore festival in Prague helps to celebrate the country's rich culture.

CULTURAL PRESERVATION

The Czechs have a lot to offer the future. Some of the world's best-known artists, writers and musicians come from this region. The government has done its best to keep the arts afloat during the economic crisis.

The Czech Republic is supposed to use at least 1 percent of the state budget for cultural preservation, regardless of which political party is in power. Unfortunately, this goal has never been reached. The amount given to the arts has only decreased since the recession. In 2010, the amount allocated to the arts was only about 0.6 percent. Overall budget cuts have also affected this situation, reducing the total amount of money to be drawn from.

The Natural Cultural Policy 2009-2014 was approved in 2008 as a road to improvement. Under this new policy, the arts were to be treated as any other discipline. This means that culture would be officially recognized as worth the time and effort that would be required to improve it. The government also offers scholarships to students wishing to pursue the arts as a career. This new policy has not been around long enough to see the lasting effects. However, the fact that these policies are being created means that the government is taking the problem very seriously. There is hope for the future.

Czech crafts displayed for Prague's Easter markets.

Power plants like this one in Pocerady contribute to the Czech Republic's high level of air pollution.

The Environment

The Czech Republic suffers from air, water, and land pollution caused by industry, mining, and agriculture. Lung cancer is common in areas with the highest air pollution levels. In the mid-1990s, the nation had the world's highest carbon dioxide emissions, totaling 135.6 million metric tons per year. The country also had its air contaminated by sulfur dioxide emissions from the use of lignite as an energy source in the former Czechoslovakia. Other Western nations have offered the Czech Republic $1 billion to spur environmental reforms, but the pressure to continue economic growth has postponed the government's push for environmental action.

Poor air quality is a major problem in the country. Acid rain has destroyed much of the forest in the northern part of the region. Farming and mining have also caused land erosion.

Catching Up

As of 2012, the Czech Republic had not set a date to launch the euro as its official currency.

Officials have stated that fixing the country's economic structure is currently a bigger priority. Adopting the euro could help improve the economy through increased trade with other member countries of the Eurozone, although the future of the euro itself is somewhat in doubt as the EU shoulders through the recent recession.

The EU is also committed to environmental protection, and once again, the Czech Republic lags behind. The European Union aims to have 20 percent of all energy within the EU come from renewable energy sources. The Czech Republic is far behind this goal, with less than 10 percent coming from RES as of 2008. Almost 60 percent of energy within this nation comes from coal, which takes a heavy toll on the environment. Another 30 percent comes from nuclear plants, which also present dangers to the environment. The Czech Republic hopes to have at least 13 percent of all energy come from renewable sources by 2020.

The Czech Republic has a long way to go to catch up with the rest of the European Union. But it has come a long way in a short time. There's hope for its future!

Time Line

400 BCE	Celts occupy Czech lands.
600 CE	Slavic peoples fully inhabit the region.
900	The Przemyslid family begins to establish the Bohemian Kingdom.
1355	Prague becomes the new Imperial city for the Holy Roman Empire.
1526	The Hapsburg Dynasty takes control of the Bohemian throne.
1914	World War I begins.
1918	Czechoslovakia proclaims itself an independent democratic state.
1938	Czechoslovakia surrenders the Sudetenland to Germany.
1939	Hitler invades the remainder of Czechoslovakia.
1945	Czechoslovakia is liberated from Nazi occupation and reestablishes democratic rule.
1948	Soviets cement communist control of Czechoslovakia.
1968	The Prague Spring reform movement is put down by Soviet troops.
1989	The Velvet Revolution takes hold and communist rule ends.
1990	First free elections held since 1942.
1993	The Czech Republic separates from the former Czechoslovakia.
2003	Czechs pass a referendum supporting membership in the EU.
2004	The Czech Republic is admitted to the EU.
2008	World recession begins.

FURTHER READING/INTERNET RESOURCES

Dowling, Maria. *Czechoslovakia*. London: Arnold Publishers, 2002.

Leff, Carol Skalnik. *The Czech and Slovak Republics: Nation Versus State.* Boulder, Colo.: Westview Press, 1996.

Roberts, Jack L. *Oskar Schindler.* Farmington Hills, Mich.: Thomson Gale, 2000.

Roux, Lindy. *Czech Republic.* Milwaukee, Wis.: Gareth Stevens Audio, 2003.

Steves, Rick, and Honza Vihan. *Rick Steves' Prague and the Czech Republic 2005.* Emeryville, Calif.: Avalon Travel Publishing, 2005.

Travel Information
www.czechtourism.com

History and Geography
www.radio.cz/en
www.worldinfozone.com/country.php?country=CzechRepublic

Culture and Festivals
www.expats.cz
www.czechtourism.com
www.czechsite.com

Economic and Political Information
www.answers.com/topic.economy-of-the-czech-republic
www.cia.gov/library/publications/the-world-factbook/geos/ez.html

EU Information
europa.eu.int/

Publisher's note:
The websites listed on this page were active at the time of publication. The publisher is not responsible for websites that have changed their addresses or discontinued operation since the date of publication. The publisher will review and update the website list upon each reprint.

FOR MORE INFORMATION

Embassy of the Czech Republic
3900 Spring of Freedom St. NW
Washington, DC, 20008
Tel.: 202-274-9100
www.mzv.cz

Embassy of the United States in Prague
Trziste 15
11801 Praha 1
The Czech Republic
Tel.: 420-257-530-663
www.usembassy.cz

European Union
Delegation of the European Commission to the United States
2300 M Street, NW
Washington, DC 20037
Tel.: 202-862-9500
Fax: 202-429-1766

Ministry of Foreign Affairs of the Czech Republic
Loretánské námìstí 5
11800 Praha 1
The Czech Republic
www.mfa.cz

Publisher's note:
The websites listed on this page were active at the time of publication. The publisher is not responsible for websites that have changed their addresses or discontinued operation since the date of publication. The publisher will review and update the Web-site list upon each reprint.

GLOSSARY

absolute rule: A government in which the monarch has complete control and does not need to consult advisers.

Age of Enlightenment: An eighteenth-century movement that led away from religious explanation for things and toward a more scientific approach to the world.

agrarian: Related to farming or rural life.

alternative medicine: The treatment of illness using remedies outside mainstream medicine.

autonomous: Able to act independently.

ceded: Gave up land rights or power to another country or group.

centralization: The concentration of political power in a central authority.

communist: A supporter of the political and social theory in which all property of a classless society is owned by all the members of the community.

compulsory: Required.

crusaders: Those who campaign hard either for or against something.

discrimination: Unfair treatment of a minority group, based on race, sex, religion, or some other difference.

elite: A small group within a larger group who have more power, social standing, or wealth than the rest of the group.

feudal: Relating to the legal and social system of medieval Europe, where vassals held land in exchange for military service.

fief: A piece of land given to someone by a feudal lord in return for service.

gross domestic product (GDP): The total value of all goods and services produced within a country in a year.

ideals: Standards of perfection.

infrastructure: A country's large-scale public systems, services, and facilities that are necessary for economic growth and development.

liberalization: The relaxation of restrictions and granting of more freedoms.

nationalism: A feeling of extreme devotion to one nation and its interests above all others.

navigable: Deep and wide enough to allow safe passage of ships.

neutral: Not belonging to or favoring any side in a dispute.

nobility: Aristocratic social position or rank.

parliament: A legislative body.

per capita: For each person.

pretext: A misleading or untrue reason given for doing something.

privatize: To transfer to private ownership something that was owned by the government.

prejudice: Fear and hatred of a group of people.

Protestant Reformation: A movement begun in the late 1500s to reform the Catholic Church.

radical: Extreme, often quick, change.

recession: A period of decline in economic trade and prosperity that is of shorter duration than a depression.

referendum: A vote by an entire electorate on a specific question or questions put before it by a government.

reneged: Went back on a promise or commitment.

satellite nation: A country completely under the control of another.

serfs: Agricultural workers of feudal Europe who were bought and sold with the land.

solidarity: Harmony of interests and responsibilities among individuals in a group.

sovereignty: Supreme authority.

Sudetenland: Region in northern Czech Republic's Sudetes Mountains.

theology: The study of religion and God's relationship to the world.

Transparency: Visibility and openness regarding information and practices.

tribute: Payment made by one ruler or state to another as a sign of submission.

INDEX

PICTURE CREDITS

About the Authors and the Consultant

Authors

Heather Docalavich first developed an interest in the history and cultures of Eastern Europe through her work as a genealogy researcher. She currently resides in Hilton Head, South Carolina, with her four children.

Shaina Carmel Indovino is a writer and illustrator living in Nesconset, New York. She graduated from Binghamton University, where she received degrees in sociology and English. Shaina has enjoyed the opportunity to apply both of her fields of study to her writing and she hopes readers will benefit from taking a look at the countries of the world through more than one perspective.

Series Consultant

Ambassador John Bruton served as Irish Prime Minister from 1994 until 1997. As prime minister, he helped turn Ireland's economy into one of the fastest-growing in the world. He was also involved in the Northern Ireland Peace Process, which led to the 1998 Good Friday Agreement. During his tenure as Ireland's prime minister, he also presided over the European Union presidency in 1996 and helped finalize the Stability and Growth Pact, which governs management of the euro. Before being named the European Commission Head of Delegation in the United States, he was a member of the convention that drafted the European Constitution, signed October 29, 2004.

The European Commission Delegation to the United States represents the interests of the European Union as a whole, much as ambassadors represent their countries' interests to the U.S. government. Matters coming under European Commission authority are negotiated between the commission and the U.S. administration.